ISLAND HERITAGE
P U B L I S H I N G

94-411 KŌ‘AKI STREET, WAIPAHU, HAWAI‘I 96797

Orders: (800) 468-2800

Info: (808) 564-8800

Fax: (808) 564-8877

www.islandheritage.com

ISBN#: 0-89610-018-9

First Edition, Sixth Printing – 2002

The Story of Hina

Written by Patrick Ching

Illustrated by Pat Hall

To teachers, parents, and smart kids

The story of Hina is based on a true story. It is an enjoyable way for children to learn about the habits and life cycle of Hawai'i's endangered monk seals.

For a more in-depth look at this beloved mammal, be sure to read *The Hawaiian Monk Seal*, by Patrick Ching. Among the main points Ching makes in this book is the importance of not disturbing the seals so that they continue to visit the main Hawaiian Islands where they can be enjoyed and appreciated for generations to come.

Happy reading...

DEDICATION

To all of Hawai'i's precious animals
and the people who care for them.

With aloha,
Patrick Ching

Makuahine (Mother) Monk Seal was especially hungry these days. She ate everything she could catch. Her menu included goodies like fish, eels, lobsters and octopus — so *ono* (delicious)! These sea creatures came out mostly at night so that's when she did most of her hunting. Makuahine Monk Seal weighed nearly 600 pounds. She needed to eat a lot. After all, she was eating for two.

After Makuahine Monk Seal had been out at sea for several weeks, nature called her to shore.

She came to an island that she had visited several times, where humans had treated her with respect and she did not fear them. She looked for a spot on the beach where she felt safe and comfortable and hauled her robust body up onto the sand. **SLOSH-KABOOM! SLOSH-KABOOM!** The ground shook as she bounced across the beach. With a *"snort"* and a *"humph"* she settled into the sand.

As twilight faded into night, the full moon lit the salty mist that pushed forth from the crashing waves. A rainbow of color danced upon the moist evening air. The people of the nearby town had little clue that on this night something magic was about to happen . . .

7

Morning's first light unveiled the miracle of life, and astonished beach goers could not believe their eyes . . .

8

There beside Makuahine Monk Seal was a
[je]t black pup with a birthmark in the shape of
[t]he full moon on her left hip. Makuahine Monk
[S]eal called to her baby with a deep, loving bellow —
["]BWAAH!" Baby replied with a high-pitched "BWAAAP!"

The news spread fast. People in the nearby little town were
[fa]miliar with monk seals, but they had never seen a newborn.
[I]n no time, the local newspapers and TV stations sent reporters to
[c]over the story. Townspeople called the infant seal Hina. They felt
[H]ina was a good name, since "*hina*" in Hawaiian means shiny
[g]ray, and the baby was a shiny *moonlit* gray.

9

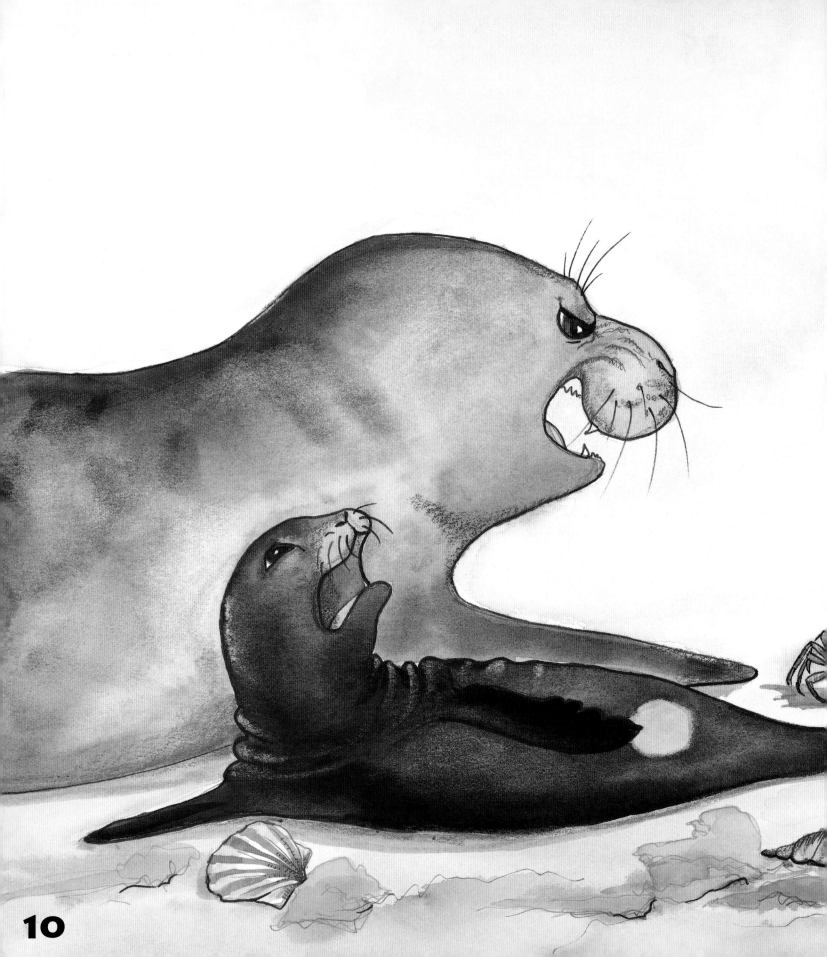

Once a couple of rowdy dogs came running up to the seals, growling and barking. Hina cried and hid behind her mother. Makuahine Monk Seal showed her teeth and growled back at the dogs. She was not afraid. Besides, a bite from an adult monk seal is like a bite from a 600-pound dog! In fact, some Hawaiians call the monk seals *'ilio-holo-kai*, which means "the dog that runs in the sea." The rowdy dogs were soon caught and taken away by the humane society officers. From then on the townspeople kept their dogs away from the seals.

The neighborhood leaders soon set up a volunteer task force to watch the new mom and pup around the clock. The volunteers made sure that curious onlookers kept their distance and did not disturb the pair. Teachers would bring their classes to visit the seals and listen as a wildlife ranger told them about the life cycle and habits of the monk seals.

The ranger told them that the seals were in danger of becoming extinct and that they lived mostly on the tiny remote Hawaiian Islands, which lie to the northwest of the main islands. The ranger also reminded the students of the importance of not disturbing the seals so that they could get their much needed rest. He said that if humans would give them their space, monk seals would be more likely to stay around the main islands and we could see them in real life ... not just in books.

Hina spent her time eating, sleeping, and playing with Makuahine Monk Seal in the waters of the shallow lagoon. Eating, sleeping, and playing . . . What a life!

Makuahine Monk Seal was very protective of her pup and did not let Hina out of her sight. She tried to show Hina how to catch fish but Hina wasn't interested. She was content with drinking the rich milk that flowed from her mother

Hina grew rapidly. Her once black fur became shiny and gray.
After a few weeks, she weighed four times what she did at birth.
Makuahine Monk Seal, however, had not eaten since Hina was born.
She grew thinner and thinner until the shape of her ribs began to
show through her skin. Makuahine Monk Seal knew it was time to
leave her pup and tend to her own nutritional needs. As night fell and
Hina lay sleeping, she slipped away into the dark ocean. Though she
cared for Hina, her job as a mother was over. Now Hina would have
to learn to take care of herself.

When morning came, Hina began to awake. Still half asleep, she reached for her mother's warm body. She opened her eyes and looked all around ... Makuahine Monk Seal was gone! Hina began to call for her mother, but her calls went unanswered. After awhile, Hina finally realized ... she was alone ...

"This is terrible!" Hina thought. "Who's going to feed me? Who's going to protect me? And most importantly ... who's going to play with me?"

Hina decided to take action. For the first time in her young life, she ventured into the deep water beyond the reef in search of Makuahine Monk Seal. In the distance she could see a shape.

"It must be mother!" she thought. "I'll swim up and surprise her."

When Hina got near, the shape became clear. It wasn't Makuahine Monk Seal but a happy little character named Nicky Nai'a. Nicky was a spinner dolphin. Nai'a is the Hawaiian word for dolphin.

"I'm looking for my mom," said Hina. "She's lost."

Nicky chuckled, "Your mama isn't lost. She's gone to take care of herself . . . and now it's time for you to do the same."

Then Nicky added, "Come with me. There's someone I'd like you to meet."

20

Hina followed Nicky Nai'a along the reef and through a maze of sea caves.

"I'd like you to meet Henry Honu," said Nicky. "Honu is the Hawaiian word for sea turtle. Henry has been on his own since the day he was hatched. He **never** got to see his mama."

"How did you eat and who did you play with?" asked Hina.

"I just did what came naturally," answered Henry Honu.

Hina thought about this. *Just what is the natural thing to do?* she wondered. It was a question that Hina would have to figure out soon enough.

With each passing day, Hina got thinner and hungrier.

The blubber that she gained from drinking her mother's milk was slowly being used to nourish her body. The "natural thing" to do was now very clear to her. Instead of playing, she had to think about a more serious pastime ... finding food!

But *what* to eat? Hina thought. She remembered the days of playing in the shallow lagoon with Makuahine Monk Seal. "Mama used to toss live sea creatures at me ... I bet that was food."

It was worth a try. Hina tried to catch anything that swam, but most of the fish were too quick for her.

Then she turned to an easier prey ... a sea cucumber. She approached the sluglike creature on the sandy ocean floor and bit into it.

"YUCK!" Hina squealed. Her face was covered with the stringy white stuff that sea cucumbers squirt when they're attacked

Hina did not give up, but continued trying and soon became a good hunter. Among her favorite foods were delicacies like fish, lobsters, eels, and octopus. She found it easier to hunt at night because that's when most of the sea animals came out.

Hina spent her nights catching food, and her days on the shore getting some much needed rest.

One day a man saw Hina resting.

"She must be sick," he thought. The man started clapping his hands and chased Hina into the water.

Hina was angry. "Why can't they just let me rest?" she complained. "When I don't sleep, I can't hunt well. If I don't catch food, I'll starve."

Hina swam away and in a short while she saw a familiar shadow in the deep.

"There's Nicky Nai'a," she thought and she swam up to meet him.

Again Hina was wrong. She was staring straight down the throat of a 12-foot tiger shark and it was hungry! Tiger sharks are the Hawaiian monk seal's most dangerous predator. The shark chased Hina all over the sea — under ledges, into caves, even through a ship wreck. Hina was just about out of breath and the shark was closing in.

Rolling back its eyes, the shark opened its mouth wide to take a chomp out of Hina. Taking advantage of the shark's temporary blindness, Hina turned around and bit the shark right on the nose. The shark wailed, flailed, and bailed out of there as fast as it could. Luckily, Hina had known that a shark's nose is the most sensitive part of its body.

Hina knew that she was lucky to get away from the shark.

"Now maybe I can find a beach where people will let me rest," Hina sighed.

She found a peaceful beach and hauled her body out of the water and bounced across the sand. With a final "THUD" and "SNORT", she fell into a deep sleep. Hina began to dream about the days she spent playing with her mother. Then she dreamed of a special place where she had many friends. Not just dolphins and turtles, but friends like herself. Monk seal friends! When Hina awoke, she was sad. In her dreams she had many companions, but now she was alone.

So Hina went off in search of friends. All around her were humans, but she found no other seals. Hina decided that humans would be her friends. She followed humans along the beach, lay with them on the shore, and swam with them in the water. In the water, Hina was nimble and quick and liked to swim circles around her human friends.

Everyone loved Hina. She soon became a local celebrity and many people took photos of her.

As Hina grew, she began to play a little rougher with her human friends. Sometimes she would playfully nip at them. This would be all right if her friends were seals, however, humans have much softer skin than monk seals and a couple of people got some painful cuts from Hina's playful antics.

So the townspeople and wildlife officials called a meeting. They loved Hina, but were concerned about the future. In a couple of years Hina would be full grown.

"Getting a bite from a full grown monk seal is like getting bitten by a giant dog," reminded one biologist. "Even a playful bite could cause severe injury."

The people sadly agreed that something must be done. They came up with a plan that they felt would be best for everyone.

One morning a group of wildlife rangers went to the harbor where Hina had been spotted the night before. A ranger named Patrick went into the water and started swirling and splashing. Within a few minutes Hina popped her head up and began swirling with Patrick. They called to each other in seal talk while Patrick slowly made his way out of the water. Hina followed behind Patrick, right up to the bed of a pickup truck.

Hina was lifted into the bed of the truck and quickly taken to a waiting helicopter. The helicopter soon lifted off and headed out to sea.

"Where are they taking me in the belly of this bird?" Hina wondered, "This is a very unusual day."

The people in the helicopter kept Hina comfortable by covering her with wet towels.

Then Hina spotted an island down below. It was getting closer and closer. All she could think of was that she might never again see her friends and the island of her birth.

The helicopter landed softly on the new beach. Hina was placed on sand near the water.

"This will be home for a while," Patrick told Hina. "I think you're gonna like it."

Hina rolled into the water. "How can I like it when I'm missing my friends?" [sh]e thought. She dove deep to see what this new place was like. From out of the [bl]ue she saw shapes and shadows heading toward her.

Were they dolphins? Turtles? Sharks? Hina began to worry.

Then a smile covered her face. The shapes coming toward her were those of [ot]her monk seals coming to greet her!

Hina swam and played with the other seals all day. At last she did not feel so [a]lone. Now she was a member of the monk seal society! She even ran into [Tū]akuahine Monk Seal and they reminisced about old times. Hina was happy in [he]r new home.

The years went by and Hina grew to maturity. She swam, ate and rested. [Sh]e molted her skin each year. She avoided sharks and drift nets and [ev]entually found a mate.

Aloha, I'm Patrick Ching. The last time I saw Hina she didn't have time to talk. She was busy eating everything in sight. The full moon made hunting good and I noticed she was especially hungry. After all, now she was eating for two.

THE END